the hospitable
DESERT

BY
PAUL BENNETT

BIRDS OF THE DESERT

Many different species of birds are found in deserts. In the deserts of North America, birds such as the cactus wren live in nest-holes or branches of the spiny, tree-like cacti that grow there. The thorn-studded plants give protection from snakes and other predators that might eat the young birds in the nest.

THE SUN-SCORCHED EARTH

Many of the deserts of the world are large. Together they cover over a quarter of the Earth's land surface. This is the Namib Desert, which covers one-third of Namibia and stretches 800 miles (1,290 km) along the coast of southwestern Africa. It receives less than 0.5 inch (1.3 cm) of rainfall a year.

ARMOR PLATED

Scorpions are particularly abundant in desert regions. They hide by day and hunt by night, using their powerful pincers to crush the insects and spiders on which they prey. Their long tails end with a stinger that they use to defend themselves.

HOPPING AROUND

Like many desert animals, this little hopping mouse avoids the searing heat of the day. It emerges from its burrow after dark when it is cooler and safer to hop about looking for food. Desert mice and rats are extremely important to life in the desert, as they are prey to a wide number of the larger animals, including owls, snakes, and foxes.

THE HOSPITABLE DESERT

It is midday. Directly overhead the sun burns fiercely in a cloudless sky. The glare is so strong that without sunglasses it makes your eyes hurt. The parched ground stretches out all around you. In the distance the rocks shimmer from the intense heat. All is silent. Nothing moves. The desert is lifeless. Or is it? At first sight, the sun-baked land of the desert is a barren place unable to support any kind of animal or plant life whatsoever. But, in fact, most deserts have an abundance of life – the animals are simply avoiding the hottest time of the day. Wait until the sun is lower in the sky and the heat has lessened, and you will see the desert begin to stir. So even though you would find the desert a hellish place to live, it is home to many animals and plants, specially adapted to the harsh conditions.

DESERTS OF THE WORLD

This map indicates the desert regions of the world by yellow shading. Most have a very hot climate, but a few that lie outside of the tropics are cool. Both arid and semi-arid regions have low rainfall. The arid regions have an annual rainfall of less than 10 inches (25 cm), and often much less. Semi-arid regions receive between 10-20 inches (25-50 cm).

LIVING IN THE DESERT

This woman is from the Tuareg tribe, a group of people from Africa's vast Sahara Desert. They are nomads, moving from place to place looking for grazing grounds for their herds. The Tuaregs keep sheep and goats, and use camels to carry water and provide milk. Most humans cannot live easily in the desert conditions, yet desert tribes have adapted to the hardships and prospered. Over many centuries they have learned how to use the land, plants, and animals to survive.

WEATHER & CLIMATE

Deserts are places where no one knows for certain when it will rain next. Months and even years may pass between rainfalls. And in some desert areas, such as in the Atacama Desert of South America, it may never rain at all. This lack of rain contributes to the dryness of the deserts, which is often made worse by the hot, dry winds that blow over them. In the daytime, the ground temperature can soar to over 176 °F (80 °C). In these conditions, a light shower of rain from passing clouds instantly evaporates before it touches the ground, and the precious rainfall is lost. As the sun sets, the temperature drops sharply because there are no clouds to stop the heat from escaping into the sky. As a result, it is not unusual for deserts to be frosty at night. Thus deserts have the biggest temperature ranges in any one day.

COLD DESERTS

Some deserts are among the coldest places on Earth. In extreme Arctic areas (above) it is the cold, rather than the heat and lack of moisture, that make it difficult for life to survive. Water is locked up in snow and ice. In tundra regions, vast treeless zones of the far north where the subsoil is permanently frozen, there is a brief summer when some of the snow melts, and plants and animals can get the water they need to flourish and reproduce.

UNDER A CLOUDLESS SKY

From space, the Atacama Desert of South America can be clearly seen. This desert is sandwiched between the Andes, the mountain chain that runs down the entire west coast of the continent, and the Pacific Ocean. The Andes act as a barrier to rain-bearing clouds blown across from the west. In addition, the effect of the Humboldt Current, a cold sea current that flows along the coastal edge of South America, is to dry the sea air before it reaches the land. This desert is one of the driest regions in the world.

DUST DEVIL

A miniature whirlwind whips up dust and sand into the air. Dust and sand storms are common whenever the wind blows strongly over the open desert. A storm blowing sand over 9,800 ft (3,000 meters) high can suddenly appear on the horizon and engulf everything almost without warning. The dust or sand is so thick that not even the glaring desert sun can be seen through it.

DESERT SAND

The great, constantly shifting dunes are formed by the wind, making it virtually impossible for any desert plant to take root and grow. Sandy deserts are not as common as other types – deserts covered by rocks and stones make up three-quarters of the world's deserts. These sand dunes in Namibia are among the tallest in the world, reaching heights of 1,200 ft (370 meters).

FLASH FLOOD

Rainfall can happen very suddenly in some desert regions. Sometimes the rain is so torrential that it may last for hours, even days. The massive amounts of water cover the land, cascade over rocks, and fill deep ravines. The water often gouges out deep channels as it moves, carrying tons of sand and rocks with it. Flash floods usually occur in the mountain regions of deserts. The water may travel many miles from the site of the rainfall.

GHOST TOWN

This abandoned building is in the once-thriving diamond mining town of Kolmanskop, in Namibia. Although the desert sand has all but swallowed up the town, buildings and items, such as machinery, cars, beds, and tables, are likely to remain intact for hundreds of years. This is because the desert has a preserving effect. The lack of moisture means that wood, leather, fiber and other natural materials do not perish or rot away, and metal does not rust and crumble into dust. Thus, deserts have a long memory – the abandoned signs of human activity scar the environment for many generations unless or until they are removed.

DESERTS OF THE WORLD

Deserts are found across the world, but most are found in belts between the Tropics of Cancer and Capricorn, in areas where the strong sun and hot wind bring little rain. The Sahara and Kalahari Deserts of Africa are of this type. Deserts are also found in the shelter of mountain ranges, such as the North American deserts of the Great Basin and Mojave. They are called rainshadow deserts because as the moist winds cross the mountains, they lose their moisture in the form of rain. By the time the winds reach the plains beyond the mountain peaks, there is little or no moisture left. The desert of central Australia and the Gobi Desert of Asia exist because they are too far from the sea – the rain-carrying winds simply never reach them.

DESERT HOMES

This thatched granary stands in a village in the Thar Desert of India. The villagers have learned how to make the best use of any rainfall. One way is to build walls around their fields, so that the rain water will not rush over the land and erode the soil. The walls trap the water, allowing it to soak into the ground and feed the plants.

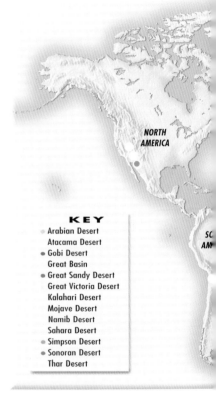

NORTH
AMERICA

SC
AM

KEY
- Arabian Desert
- Atacama Desert
- Gobi Desert
- Great Basin
- Great Sandy Desert
- Great Victoria Desert
- Kalahari Desert
- Mojave Desert
- Namib Desert
- Sahara Desert
- Simpson Desert
- Sonoran Desert
- Thar Desert

MONUMENT VALLEY

This spectacular desert area on the Arizona-Utah border in the United States is a rock desert that was formed by erosion over millions of years. The cliff-like rock formations, called buttes, which are hundreds of feet high, are made from sandstone. The rock is worn away by the wind and, occasionally, water. The valley floor itself is bare and flat, and is strewn with the broken fragments and fine particles of the rock slabs of fallen buttes.

DESERTS LONG AGO

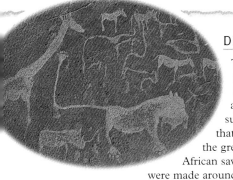

These beautiful rock paintings show that the Sahara region was once a less arid place, able to support those animals that are found today on the great grassy plains of the African savanna. The drawings were made around 5,000 years ago, when the climate of North Africa was much wetter. As the climate changed and the weather became hotter, the lakes and water holes slowly began to dry out, creating the desert we know today.

THE SAHARA DESERT

The Sahara Desert in North Africa is the largest desert in the world. It covers almost a third of the African continent, and is almost the size of the United States. The great camel caravans seen on the Sahara are usually controlled by the Tuaregs, who traditionally traveled across vast areas of the desert, even up to the Mediterranean, to trade. But not all of the Sahara is sand. The sandy regions, called ergs, only make up one-fifth of the area – the rest is made up of mountains, stony plateaus, and dust-filled basins.

EUROPE

ASIA

PACIFIC OCEAN

AFRICA

ATLANTIC OCEAN

INDIAN OCEAN

AUSTRALIA

THE SIMPSON DESERT

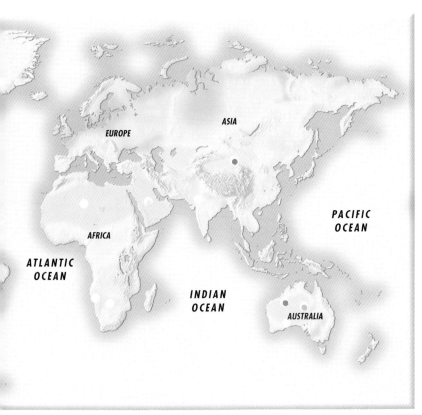

The Simpson Desert is a region of about 56,000 sq miles (145,000 sq km) in central Australia. Here sand dunes up to 115 ft (35 meters) high and 1,500 ft (450 meters) apart run parallel across the desert. In between these sand-dune crests grows spinifex grass, which is specially adapted to the dry desert conditions. The Simpson Desert is home to some of the most unique desert animals, such as marsupial mice, but these have become threatened since the introduction of the cat to Australia.

DESERT PLANTS

Plants have evolved special ways of living in the desert. Only the shifting sand dunes are plant free, as it is impossible for the plants to establish themselves. But elsewhere, plants are able to exist, and have adapted in a variety of ways. They have to survive long periods of drought. The rain, when it comes, is unpredictable – it could be a light shower or it could fall in torrents. Many plants deal with these extremes by using every drop of moisture they can take up in their roots, storing it in their stems or in underground tubers (fleshy roots).

ANNUAL PLANTS

In the desert, some plants, such as this yellowtop, avoid the problem of the drought by remaining as seeds. When it rains, the seeds suddenly sprout and the plant grows very quickly, taking advantage of the moisture in the soil before it dries up. The plant flowers and then produces seeds ready for the next time it rains. After seeding, the plant dies.

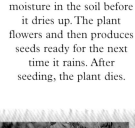

Englemann's prickly pear

CACTUS FLOWERS

Cacti produce some of the most beautiful and colorful flowers in the desert. Some cacti have only one flower at a time, while others have many. The flowers only last for a short time – from a single night in some cases to several days in others.

Claw cactus

GIANT SAGUARO CACTUS

These giant tree-like plants of the North American deserts can reach a height of 52 ft (16 meters) and a weight of 10 tons.
They send out a network of shallow roots up to 33 ft (10 meters) in all directions. The roots are strong and dense to both absorb as much water as possible and keep the plant upright in strong winds. These majestic cacti take a very long time to grow – this one may be over 200 years old.

Cacti suck up water when it rains and hoard it in their stems, using it gradually to grow during the long periods of drought. When there is another downpour, they can refill their tanks

Leaves have been reduced to spines, to minimize water loss and to protect the plant

Stem has a waxy surface to stop water loss

Ribs or pleats expand when it rains to store water in its sponge-like cells

Roots spread out near the surface to take up rain water

TUNISIAN OASIS

Oases are natural springs fed by water that comes from a distant source, such as rain-fed mountains, maybe hundreds of miles away. The water flows underground through the rock until the rock comes to the surface. Desert people settle by oases as the surrounding area is very fertile. There, plants and trees flourish, such as these palms, which are harvested for dates. In Australia, oases are called billabongs.

CREOSOTE BUSH

This bush, so called because of its odor, flourishes when there is lots of space around it. It spreads its roots and absorbs the moisture that has collected a few inches below the surface of the soil. It gleans the water so effectively that no other plants can grow within several feet of it. The waxy coating on the leaves helps to reduce water loss.

DESERT OAKS

These trees in the Simpson Desert of Australia send down long roots, called tap roots, deep in the soil in search of water. A network of roots at every level ensures that the trees capture every drop of moisture that is in the soil. Plants that grow on valley floors often use this method to absorb water. Tap roots may grow tens of feet in order to reach an underground water supply.

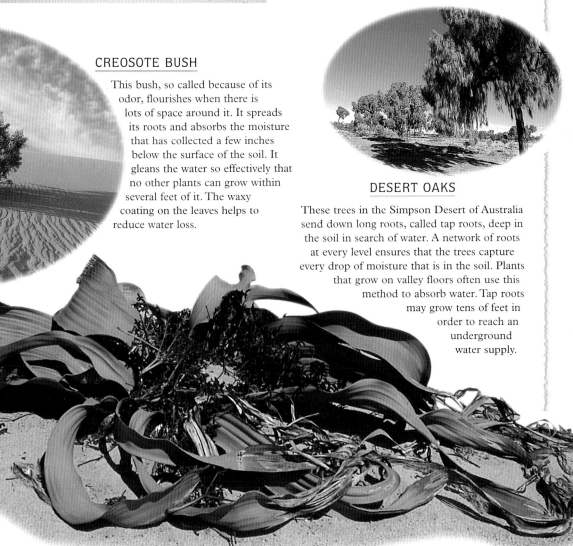

WELWITSCHIA

This unusual-looking plant grows in the Namib Desert. The Namib borders the coast and at night a fog often rolls in from the sea, leaving drops of moisture on the ground and on the plants. The Welwitschia has a fat, swollen root, from which grow long, strap-like leaves that can absorb water droplets. Any water that is not taken up runs off the leaves to be collected by the plant's roots.

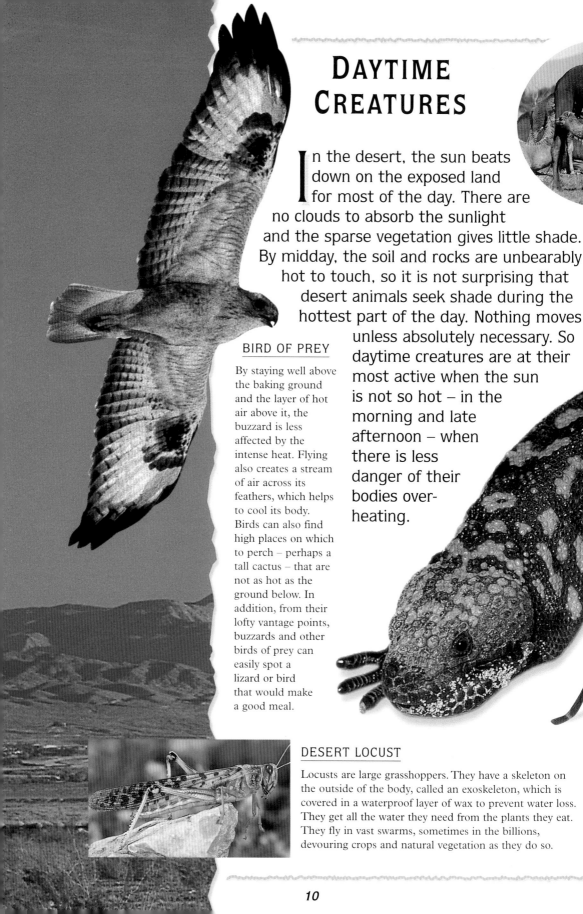

DAYTIME CREATURES

I n the desert, the sun beats down on the exposed land for most of the day. There are no clouds to absorb the sunlight and the sparse vegetation gives little shade. By midday, the soil and rocks are unbearably hot to touch, so it is not surprising that desert animals seek shade during the hottest part of the day. Nothing moves unless absolutely necessary. So daytime creatures are at their most active when the sun is not so hot – in the morning and late afternoon – when there is less danger of their bodies over-heating.

BIRD OF PREY

By staying well above the baking ground and the layer of hot air above it, the buzzard is less affected by the intense heat. Flying also creates a stream of air across its feathers, which helps to cool its body. Birds can also find high places on which to perch – perhaps a tall cactus – that are not as hot as the ground below. In addition, from their lofty vantage points, buzzards and other birds of prey can easily spot a lizard or bird that would make a good meal.

DESERT LOCUST

Locusts are large grasshoppers. They have a skeleton on the outside of the body, called an exoskeleton, which is covered in a waterproof layer of wax to prevent water loss. They get all the water they need from the plants they eat. They fly in vast swarms, sometimes in the billions, devouring crops and natural vegetation as they do so.

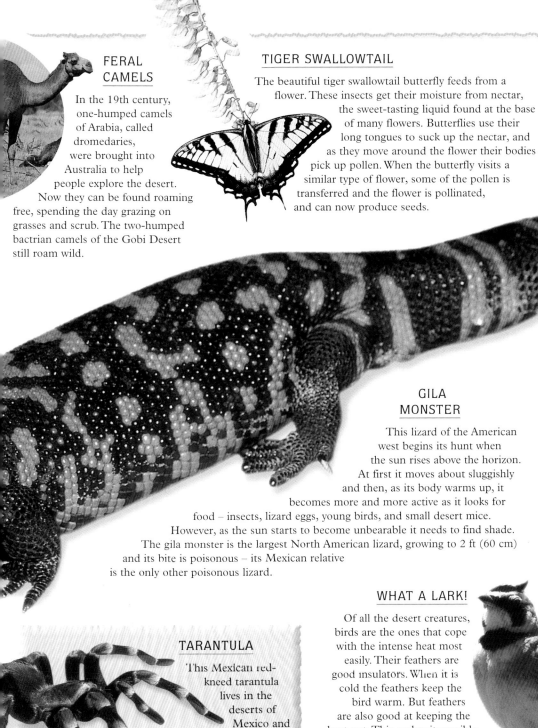

FERAL CAMELS

In the 19th century, one-humped camels of Arabia, called dromedaries, were brought into Australia to help people explore the desert. Now they can be found roaming free, spending the day grazing on grasses and scrub. The two-humped bactrian camels of the Gobi Desert still roam wild.

TIGER SWALLOWTAIL

The beautiful tiger swallowtail butterfly feeds from a flower. These insects get their moisture from nectar, the sweet-tasting liquid found at the base of many flowers. Butterflies use their long tongues to suck up the nectar, and as they move around the flower their bodies pick up pollen. When the butterfly visits a similar type of flower, some of the pollen is transferred and the flower is pollinated, and can now produce seeds.

GILA MONSTER

This lizard of the American west begins its hunt when the sun rises above the horizon. At first it moves about sluggishly and then, as its body warms up, it becomes more and more active as it looks for food – insects, lizard eggs, young birds, and small desert mice. However, as the sun starts to become unbearable it needs to find shade. The gila monster is the largest North American lizard, growing to 2 ft (60 cm) and its bite is poisonous – its Mexican relative is the only other poisonous lizard.

TARANTULA

This Mexican red-kneed tarantula lives in the deserts of Mexico and the southern USA. It hides in its silk-lined nest for most of the day and then emerges in the afternoon, using its long, hairy legs to run down its prey, which are mainly beetles and other insects. It uses poisoned fangs to kill its food and protect itself from attack.

WHAT A LARK!

Of all the desert creatures, birds are the ones that cope with the intense heat most easily. Their feathers are good insulators. When it is cold the feathers keep the bird warm. But feathers are also good at keeping the heat out. This makes it possible for birds to sit in the desert sun without overheating. When birds get too hot, they reduce their temperature by fluttering their throats. This desert lark is active throughout most of the day.

NIGHTTIME CREATURES

As darkness falls, the temperature begins to drop. Cold-blooded creatures (animals unable to make heat to warm their bodies, such as lizards) loose their warmth quickly and so must retire to their burrows when it gets too cold.

However, for most desert creatures the coolness is a welcome relief from the stifling heat, and they stir from their daytime slumber as the sun begins to set. For them the hours of darkness are the best time to be active. Small mammals, such as desert mice, move about timidly looking for seeds and bits of dead vegetation to eat. By dawn, the ground and rocks will have lost nearly all the stored heat from the previous day. This is the coldest time of the day, and many of the nocturnal animals return to their holes and crevices. Soon the day-shift creatures will be on the move, often led by the birds, which are the desert's early risers.

EASTERN SCREECH OWL

Like most owls, this bird is nocturnal. It is a bird of prey – it hunts other animals for food – and stays comfortable in its nest-hole during the day, conserving its energy. But as night falls, it leaves its home to search for the mice, insects, and lizards that become active after dark. The screech owl is well adapted to hunting at night. Extremely good eyesight and very sensitive hearing enable it to locate its prey. Its feathers help it to stay warm in the cold hours of darkness.

NIGHTTIME TRACKS

Sometimes the only evidence of night-time creatures is their tracks in the sand.

FENNEC FOX   **SIDEWINDER SNAKE**   **KANGAROO RAT**

KANGAROO RAT

This small mammal from North America stays in its burrow during the day to escape the heat. At night it forages for seeds, from where it gets its water, as well as its food. This highly adapted animal is also able to make water in its body as it digests food. To retain moisture, its breath is cooled in the passages of its nose, so that any water particles in its breath are condensed and passed back into the body. Like many other desert creatures its droppings are hard and dry.

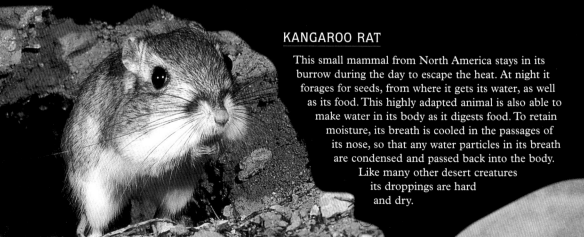

NIGHT-HUNTING GECKO

Although most lizards are daytime hunters, not all lizards retire to their crevices as soon as the sun goes down – as long as the earth and rocks still retain some warmth, they are able to continue to hunt for food. This gecko is from the deserts of central Asia. It grows to 8 inches (20 cm) in length, and lives in a burrow.

HOTSON'S FIVE-TOED JERBOA

The jerboa can be found in the Sahara Desert. It has short, weak forelimbs, long hind limbs, and a long tail, making it look like a small kangaroo. It ventures out of its nest as soon as night falls, in the hope that the darkness will give it some protection from fennec foxes and other enemies. As the jerboa hops about, it looks for seeds, tufts of grass, and other bits and pieces of plants that make up its diet. Some of its food may have blown into its area by the wind.

FENNEC FOX

These hunters of the Sahara Desert have large triangular ears for picking up the sounds made by gerbils and other small animals as they scamper around the desert looking for food. Fennec foxes move silently, their noses to the ground, sniffing for a scent trail that may lead to a tasty meal. Its large eyes help it to see in the darkness of the night.

FINDING WATER

Water is essential for life – it replaces lost fluids and is vital for many body processes. So how are desert creatures able to survive the hot, dry conditions that can last for months, or even years, before there is even a drop of rain? The answer is that they have all found ways of conserving water. A few of them do not even need to drink. They either get what little water they need from their food or they make it in their bodies as part of the process of turning food into body fuel. Birds have the advantage of being able to fly to a source of water. Other animals make long journeys to find the water they need.

A WATER CARRIER

Sand grouse build their nests up to 25 miles (40 km) from a pool. When the eggs hatch, the males ferry water back to their chicks in their feathers. As they paddle in the pool, their breast feathers become wet, and when they are fully saturated they fly back to the nest where the chicks "suck" the water off with their beaks.

WATER FROM PLANTS

Like some other large desert animals, the dorcas gazelle of Africa finds much of the water it needs from the plants it eats. The leaves contain the plants' sap, and this watery fluid is enough for the gazelle to survive.

AT THE WATER HOLE

The red kangaroo, one of the largest of the kangaroo family, is found all over Australia, including the desert regions. It gets very little water from the grasses it eats, and so the kangaroo makes a trip from its grazing grounds to a water hole every day. Red kangaroos live in herds, or mobs, of around 10 to 15 animals.

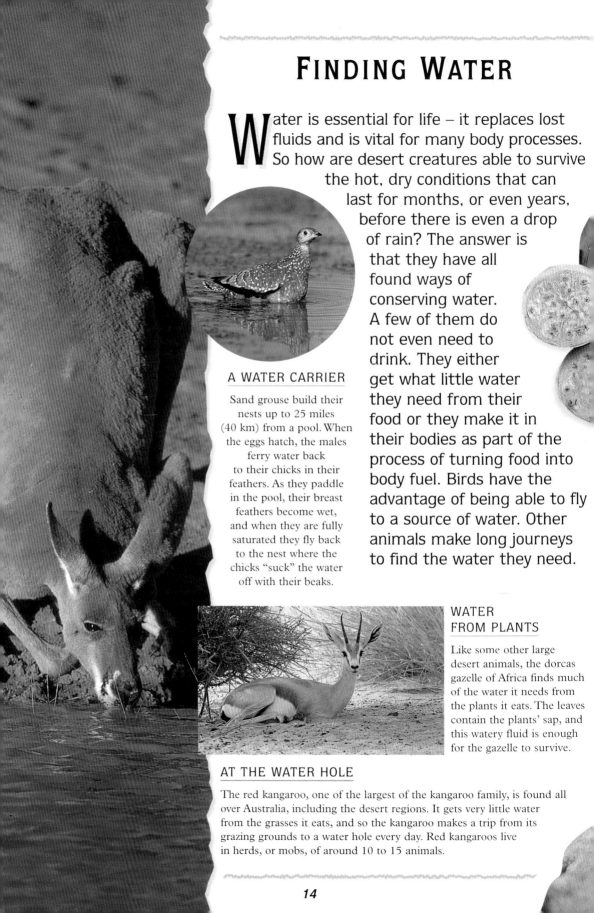

CATCHING WATER

This beetle from the Namib Desert takes advantage of the fog that often hangs over the desert at night. It climbs to the top of a sand dune and stands facing the sea with its head downwards and its body lifted up into the air. As water droplets form on its body, they roll down to the beetle's mouth and the beetle then drinks them.

FRUIT JUICE

The fruits of plants are a good source of water. These are the fruit of the prickly pear, which are moist and juicy. Birds, beetles, and other creatures that eat these fruits have little need of drinking water.

OPEN WIDE

The road runner is a bird often seen running across the deserts of North America on its slender legs. The adult bird feeds its chicks by dropping food – a lizard or snake – into the chick's gaping mouth, and in doing so trickles water from its beak into the throat of the chick, allowing it to drink.

BODY FLUIDS

The desert jackal hunts animals for food, and the kill provides it with enough water so that it does not need to make special trips to a water hole. The water is in the form of body fluids, which it swallows as it feeds. For example, blood is a body fluid, and about half of it is made up of a substance called plasma, which is mainly water.

SURVIVING THE HEAT

The best way of surviving the heat is simply to avoid it. So the majority of desert animals rest in the daytime in a cool burrow or crevice in the rocks. Those that do not go underground find shade to wait out the heat, though this can be difficult in deserts where vegetation is sparse with few leaves to cast large shadows. Even the slightest movement of a leg or the head produces heat in an animal's body, so at the hottest time of the day most animals keep as still as possible. Even lizards and snakes, which need warmth in order to be active, are at the mercy of the hot conditions. Their bodies would dangerously overheat if they stayed out in the open.

COOLING DOWN

The emu is a large flightless bird that lives in most parts of Australia, including the desert areas. They cope with the heat of the desert quite well, and when they need to cool themselves, they flutter their throats to lose heat.

WATER RETENTION

Some species of toad survive well in the desert dryness. They store up to half their body weight in water in their bladder. Desert toads are able to survive an extremely long drought in this way.

SUN SHADE

This ground squirrel is active during the daytime, taking its portable "parasol" with it wherever it goes. When it gets too hot, it erects its bushy tail over its head and spreads the hairs so that it casts as wide a shadow as possible. It cocks its tail to adjust the position of the shadow so that it always falls on its body.

GOING UNDERGROUND

This African lizard (below) is perfectly adapted to the harsh conditions found in desert dunes. It is called a sand swimmer from the way it appears to swim through the sand with fish-like movements of its body. The surface of the dune gets unbearably hot in the daytime, but just a few inches below the surface it is much cooler. The grains of sand are so smooth and dry that the lizard is able to swim through the sand to where a beetle is moving around on the surface. It then pops out to seize the beetle in its strong jaws.

WATERTIGHT SKIN

This horned viper's watertight skin allows it to retain all the water in its body.

COOL EARS

The huge ears of the North American jack rabbit act like radiators to give off heat. A fine network of blood vessels running just under the skin cool down the rabbit's body, as air blows over its ears.

Heavy tail is an aid to "swimming"

Small legs which it holds close to its body when "swimming" through the sand

Fringes on its feet allow it to run on the surface of the dune

Skin does not sweat so water is conserved

Tight-fitting scales and streamlined shape for traveling quickly through the sand

Sunken ears for smooth shape

Sharp, chisel-shaped nose for pushing the sand aside as it travels forwards

WHEN IT RAINS

FAIRY SHRIMP

Swarms of tiny fairy shrimp swim in muddy pools left by a cloudburst. They appear so fast that it is as if they had fallen with the rain. In fact, they have hatched from eggs that have been in the soil or blown on the wind since the last rain – which in some instances may be as long as 50 years ago.

They are in a hurry to grow and mate before the puddles dry out and they die. By the time all the water has gone, their eggs have been laid ready for the next generation of these tiny creatures.

For most of the year, the desert looks barren and it is a wonder that animals and plants exist there at all. Often the richness of life is a surprise, and only really becomes apparent when it rains. This is the trigger that brings the parched, dry earth to life, for there are many creatures and plants that cram all the active parts of their life cycle into one short period when water is abundant. Until the downpour, they remain dormant and unseen, but afterwards they flourish, reaching maturity with incredible speed before the puddles and lakes dry up in the unrelenting sun. Then when all the water has evaporated and the land is once again dry and parched, all that is left is their shriveled remains. But they have fulfilled their purpose – to reproduce and ensure there are future generations of life.

SPADEFOOT TOAD

The gift of water is too much to miss for the spadefoot toad, for this is the signal for the toad to emerge from the soil, where it buries itself, to mate in the pools of water. Once the eggs are laid and fertilized, the toads hop away to feed. They must build up their reserves before they again burrow into the ground to wait for the next fall of rain. In the meantime, the eggs develop very fast. Within a day or two the pool is swarming with tadpoles, which must finish their development before the pool dries out. Only a few will mature into toads and make their home in the desert.

BLOOMING DUNE

After a shower of rain the desert can become a riot of color. On the right, evening primrose plants are flowering in the shifting sand of the Sonoran Desert in the USA.

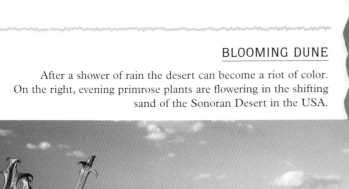

DEVIL'S CLAW SEED POD

This weird "growth" is a devil's claw seed pod. In the desert, seed heads and seed pods quickly become brown and dry, and dead looking. But as soon as there is a cloudburst, they appear to come to life, for the rainwater causes the parts to split allowing the seeds to fall to the ground and grow.

ALGAE

The dust that blows around the desert contains microscopic spores – cells that are so small that they can only be seen under a microscope. In the pools these develop into the filaments of simple plants called algae. The algae grow fast and reproduce not by mating, but by shedding more microscopic spores into the water. When the pool dries up, the algae dies. However, the spores have a tough skin and are able to withstand the hot desert conditions. They blow about the desert until the next fall of rain.

BEFORE AND AFTER

The semi-arid region of Namaqualand in South Africa is shown here before and after the rain. The picture on the right shows the dry parched landscape. The picture on the left shows the desert after the rain, when dormant seeds have suddenly burst into life.

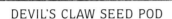

HAWK

LIZARD

BEETLE

Large birds of prey, such as the hawk, prey on smaller animals, including lizards and rodents. These feed on the many beetles and insects that live in the desert.

PREDATORS & PREY

FROM PREDATOR TO PREY

This desert cat has caught a sand viper, a poisonous snake. The snake was probably on the lookout for its own prey, perhaps a mouse, when it was caught. Carnivores are often food for other meat eaters.

F or almost any animal, the desert is a dangerous place, not only because of the heat and lack of moisture, but also because many creatures are the prey of larger animals. The most intense feeding activity occurs when the heat of the day has passed – in the late afternoon and into the evening. This is when many creatures come out of their burrows or nest holes to find food. Fortunately for both daytime and nighttime feeders most deserts have an abundance of invertebrates, such as spiders, ants, and beetles, which are the staple food for many birds, rodents, and reptiles. In turn, these become prey for the larger meat-eating predators. In the desert, most predators have adapted themselves in ingenious ways to the harsh desert conditions.

LOOKING FOR BUGS

The pointed face and spines of the desert hedgehog of North Africa are very similar to hedgehogs found in European countries. However, their ears are larger. This helps them to catch every sound in the desert. Their large ears also help them to lose heat. The desert hedgehog is always on the search for beetles and other insects on its nightly forages.

SAHARAN CHEETAH

A cheetah in West Africa runs down its prey. It can reach a speed of 60 mph (96 km/h), but only over a short distance, after which it will usually give up if it has not caught its prey. Top predators like cheetahs also provide food for scavengers like vultures and hyenas.

A THORNY DEVIL

This weird-looking creature from Australia gets its name from the thorn-like spikes that cover its body. Also called the moloch lizard, its method of feeding is to sit by a trail of ants and flick them up into its mouth using its tongue. It can eat several thousand ants at any one time. Since the ants are eaten one by one, the meal can take quite some time!

A DEADLY HUG

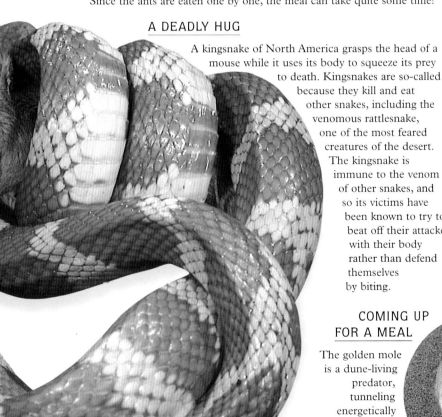

A kingsnake of North America grasps the head of a mouse while it uses its body to squeeze its prey to death. Kingsnakes are so-called because they kill and eat other snakes, including the venomous rattlesnake, one of the most feared creatures of the desert. The kingsnake is immune to the venom of other snakes, and so its victims have been known to try to beat off their attacker with their body rather than defend themselves by biting.

COMING UP FOR A MEAL

The golden mole is a dune-living predator, tunneling energetically through the sand and coming above ground to catch insects, like this locust.

FENNEC FOX

DESERT MOUSE

SEEDS

Foxes pounce on mice as they scurry around the desert looking for seeds and other plant food. Plants make their food through photosynthesis. In this way, it is the energy of the sun that begins the desert food chain.

DEFENSE

Desert animals are in a constant battle to stay alive. Part of the battle is to escape from their predators when attacked, and so they have evolved an amazing number of ways to avoid their enemies. Some of these are very simple, such as running or hopping away at high speed when threatened. The jack rabbit, for example, can reach 43 mph (70 km/h) in a series of long springing bounds when chased by a hungry coyote. Other defenses, such as camouflage, when animals simply blend into the scenery, may be less athletic but can be equally effective.

GOING UNDERGROUND

Ground squirrels found in North America and Africa build extensive networks of tunnels in which they live. In North America, they make a very loud warning "chirp" when a bird of prey soars into view before bolting for cover.

If a rattlesnake comes near, they make more warning chirps and "flag" their tails to indicate the position of the snake.

SPEED

Many animals simply flee from their attackers as fast as they can. A large predator, such as a desert fox or cat, will approach its prey by stealth, so that it can get close enough to leap. But once spotted, the prey will try to get away, with the predator giving chase. If the animal is fast enough, it will outrun its attacker and so escape.

PROTECTIVE SHELLS

Tortoises do not need speed to escape their enemies. Their defense is the armored shell they carry around with them into which they retreat when danger threatens. They withdraw their heads completely, protecting the entrances at the front and back with their scaly skin. This allows them to feed on wild flowers and other plants at their leisure.

CAMOUFLAGE

Most desert animals have a basic color pattern that suits their habitat, making them blend in with the background. But the chameleon has the added advantage of being able to vary its color, thus enhancing its camouflage to escape its enemies.

BRIGHT COLORS

In the animal world, brightly colored markings are a warning to other animals that a creature is nasty to eat or poisonous. The colors are designed to make them as obvious as possible. In the case of the coral snakes of North America, the bands of color are saying, "Keep away because I've got a poisonous bite!" As a result, most predators stay well clear of the snake and avoid attacking it.

JUST BLUFFING

Sheer bluff is the means by which this Australian frill-necked lizard repels attackers. The large photograph shows the enormous neck frill, which is the main feature of the bluff. Above shows the frill before it is spread. Below is the frill fully erected. At the same time, the lizard will also stand on its hind legs and, with its mouth wide open, bob its head and lash its tail back and forth to frighten off its predator.

NESTS, EGGS & YOUNG

RED TAIL HAWKS

These majestic daytime hunters of the North American deserts make their ragged nests high in the prickly branches of saguaro cacti. This helps to ensure that the eggs and chicks will not get dangerously hot in the unbearable heat of the day. The nest is built out of the reach of predators. At night, the warmth from the parents' bodies stops the chick from getting too cold as the temperature plummets.

Reptiles, such as lizards and snakes, generally lay their eggs and then leave. After hatching, the young must look after themselves. Amphibians, such as frogs and toads, generally make poor parents, too. After the eggs are laid in a pool of water, the adults move on. However, other animals show some form of caring for their young. Social insects, such as ants and termites that live in colonies, have workers that tend and feed the larvae until they become adult. But it is the birds and mammals that make the most effort in raising a family. Their offspring are kept clean, fed, and protected until they are old enough to fend for themselves.

MEERKATS

The meerkat, or suricate, of the desert country of southern Africa lives in community burrows. The young are born underground, but as they grow they begin to venture out as a group, and always in the company of adult meerkats. The adults keep a constant lookout for predators, and at the slightest sign of danger they give an alarm and everyone dives for the safety of the burrow.

FENNEC FOX & HER BABIES

Mammals, like this fennec fox, take excellent care of their babies. The female fox suckles her young with milk from a gland called a mammary gland. But first the mother builds an underground nest called a den, where the young will be safe from desert predators. After the babies are born, she feeds, cleans, and keeps them warm. As the babies grow, the mother gradually changes the diet from milk to solid food, bringing them desert mice to eat.

DESERT LOCUST

Like a lot of other insects, these mini-beasts show only a basic form of care for their young. The female uses her egg-laying organ, or ovipositor, to drill into the soil before laying her eggs. By placing them under-ground she hides them from hungry enemies.

HITCHING A RIDE

Scorpions are fearsome hunters but they make excellent parents. After hatching from the eggs, the young scorpions hitch a ride on their mother's back. There they are safe, protected by the mother's strong pincers and deadly sting, until they are large enough to look after themselves.

LIVING TOGETHER

Some desert animals spend their entire lives living together. In the case of insect societies, many thousands of individuals live in a colony, working together to carry out many different tasks, such as nest building, breeding and defense against enemy attack. The degree of organization of these large communities seems incredible, as they function almost like a single creature. Because of this, they are sometimes called "super organisms."

Other animals that live in groups may not have the same numbers or degree of organization, but they still depend on one another for survival.

SAFETY IN NUMBERS

A flock of ring-neck doves gather at a desert water hole to drink. There is safety in numbers for the doves, for while some of the birds are drinking, the other ones are on the lookout for enemies. This makes it very difficult for any predator to pounce on the flock by surprise.

NIGHTTIME PARTNERS

A cactobastis moth sits on a prickly pear cactus. Instead of closing their flowers at night, some desert plants do just the opposite and open them to attract the night-time insect visitors that pollinate them. In return the insects get a rewarding meal of nectar.

GEMSBOK

Herds of this stocky animal are found in the arid areas south of the Sahara Desert. The gemsbok is a type of oryx, and is well adapted to living in the desert. It feeds on dry vegetation, and can go for long periods without drinking. Its cousins once lived in large numbers in the deserts of the Sahara, and the Sinai and Arabian Peninsulas, but they were hunted to extinction. More recently, the oryx was bred in zoos and reintroduced to the wild in the 1980s.

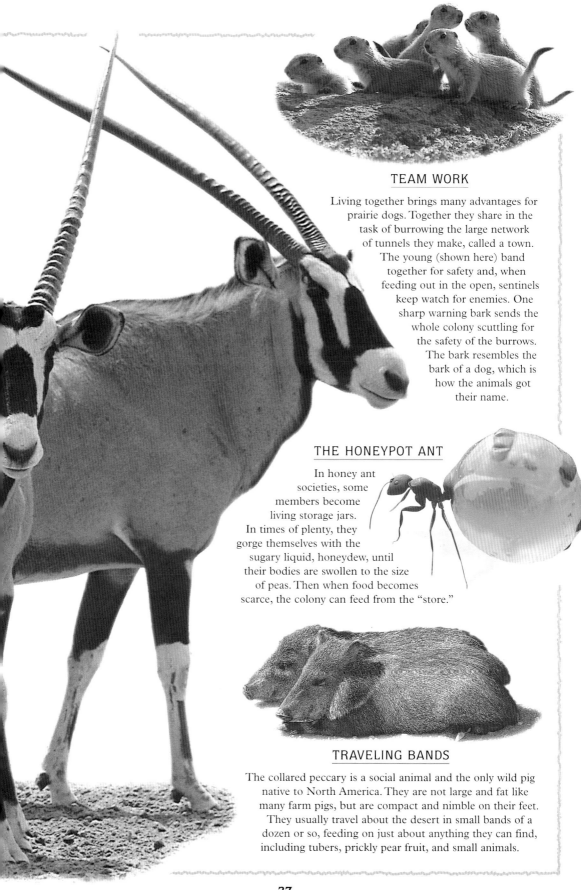

TEAM WORK

Living together brings many advantages for prairie dogs. Together they share in the task of burrowing the large network of tunnels they make, called a town. The young (shown here) band together for safety and, when feeding out in the open, sentinels keep watch for enemies. One sharp warning bark sends the whole colony scuttling for the safety of the burrows. The bark resembles the bark of a dog, which is how the animals got their name.

THE HONEYPOT ANT

In honey ant societies, some members become living storage jars. In times of plenty, they gorge themselves with the sugary liquid, honeydew, until their bodies are swollen to the size of peas. Then when food becomes scarce, the colony can feed from the "store."

TRAVELING BANDS

The collared peccary is a social animal and the only wild pig native to North America. They are not large and fat like many farm pigs, but are compact and nimble on their feet. They usually travel about the desert in small bands of a dozen or so, feeding on just about anything they can find, including tubers, prickly pear fruit, and small animals.

PEOPLE OF THE DESERT

espite the harshness of the weather conditions, people who live in the desert are able to make use of what it has to offer to support their families and make a living. For example, in North America, Native American tribes, such as the Hopi and Navajo, learned long ago to use the plants and animals of the desert for food, clothing, and shelter. And in Africa, the bushmen of the Kalahari Desert know many secrets of the desert, including which plants have tubers that store enough water to provide a drink. Without such special knowledge, people would not survive long in the harsh desert conditions.

LIVING UNDERGROUND

The Australian town of Coober Pedy is on the edge of the virtually waterless Great Victoria Desert. Most of the world's opals are mined here. Its name means "white man's hole," which refers to the practice of early miners who built their homes underground to escape the high temperatures.

PORTABLE HOMES

The nomads of the Gobi Desert of Central Asia move from one area to another in order to find enough grass for their large flocks of animals to feed on. Their homes, called yurts, can be put up, taken down, and transported very easily. The Gobi Desert is one of the largest deserts in the world, about 1,000 miles (1,600 km) long and 625 miles (1,000 km) wide.

AUSTRALIAN ABORIGINES

The Aborigines of the Australian Desert are able to supply all their needs from the land. For example, they know which different areas, whether rocky hills or sand dunes, provide the particular species of plants they require or animals to hunt. They know where the water holes are, and they reach the water in dry creek beds by digging away the sand until water seeps into the hole.

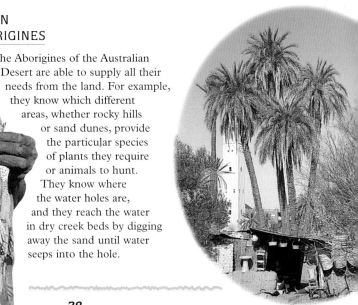

FRUITS OF THE DESERT

People living close to oases are able to irrigate the land and produce crops. Often palm trees are grown for their harvest of dates, which may be spread out on the ground to dry in the Sun.

NOMADS OF THE SAHARA

Even the great dune deserts of the Sahara are inhabited by the Tuareg, a nomadic people who lead caravans of camels with goods to trade. They carry cloth, dates, precious metals, and other goods to sell or exchange at ancient trading cities for the things they need, such as salt. The nomads wear long flowing cloaks and cover their faces to protect them from the sun.

LOCAL MATERIALS

A Moroccan basket maker displays his wares. The people of desert regions have learned to live in harmony with their environment, taking only what they need in order to survive. By using local resources wisely for producing items for sale or for building materials, they put little demand on the desert.

REFORESTATION

Reforestation projects are becoming necessary in the southern Sahara. Whole villages are becoming involved in such projects, as the trees they plant hold the soil together and prevent erosion from the wind and rain. Areas that have been cleared of trees and shrubs are replanted before they become part of the advancing desert.

SALT MINES

Walvis Bay is on the coastal margin of the Namib Desert. Here the sea water slowly evaporates in the hot sun, leaving behind a layer of sea salt. Saltpans are similar, only they form in desert basins and rely on the evaporation of rainwater for the surface cover of mineral salts. Salt is a valuable item, and in some cases the deposits are intensively mined, with disruption to the desert environment caused by the extraction itself and the transport used to take the salt away.

PROTECTING THE DESERTS

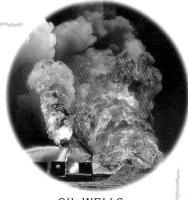

The deserts are fragile places that can easily be spoiled. For example, some of the world's greatest oilfields are found in desert areas. Although oil brings much-needed resources to the countries that extract it, the building of wells, storage tanks, oil pipelines, and roads inevitably has a harmful impact on the environment. Attempts to make the desert bloom, through irrigation schemes, have also had an adverse effect in many deserts. Desert water contains high levels of mineral salts, and these build up in the soil until no plants can grow. If the animals and plants of the desert are to survive, such as the endangered Gila monster lizard of North America, they must be protected from the thoughtless actions of people.

OIL WELLS

An oil well in Kuwait burns out of control after it was set on fire by Iraqi forces. Pollution ruined large areas of desert during the Gulf War in early 1991.

OVER GRAZING

The number of people living permanently along the desert margin has increased in recent years. The people farm the land, cutting down trees for fuel and keeping herds of grazing animals, such as goats. This has put great pressure on the already sparse vegetation, which is not given enough time to recover properly. As a result, the edge of the desert slowly advances, reducing the area for farming.

CITIES IN THE DESERT

Many cities have sprung up in desert regions, such as Las Vegas in the Nevada Desert in the USA, famous for its luxury hotels and casinos. The inhabitants of desert cities live and work in air-conditioned buildings. The huge supply of water a city demands cannot usually be met locally. So it must be piped in from rivers or reservoirs perhaps hundreds of miles away. A good road network encourages more and more people to visit the desert, diminishing the areas that are left unspoiled.

THE SPREADING DESERT

Along the margins of many deserts are zones of semi-desert. These zones are not true desert, but regions where the rainfall is enough for crops to grow. As more people settle in these areas to farm the land, these areas are turning into desert due to poor farming techniques. The map shows the risk of desertification in northwest Africa. The problem was made worse by a severe drought from 1969 to 1973. This led to the first ever United Nations conference on desertification in 1977.

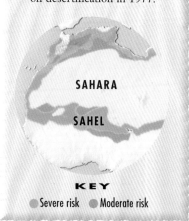

SAHARA

SAHEL

KEY

● Severe risk ● Moderate risk

FIND OUT MORE

Useful Addresses and Websites

To find out more about arid regions, or the protection of desert wildlife, here are some organizations who may be able to help.

ARIZONA-SONORA DESERT MUSEUM
2021 N. Kinney Road, Tucson, AZ 85743-8918
(520) 883-1380 http://www.desert.museum.org/

DESERT FISHES COUNCIL
P.O. Box 337, Bishop, CA 93515
(760) 872-8751

DESERT SURVIVOR
P.O. Box 20991, Oakland, CA 94620-0991
bighorn@desert-survivors.org

THE LIVING DESERT
47-900 Portola Avenue, Palm Beach, CA 92260
(760) 346-5694

SIERRA CLUB
85 Second Street, Second Floor,
San Francisco, CA 94105-3441
(415) 977-5500

UNITED NATIONS ENVIRONMENT PROGRAM (UNEP)
Information and Public Affairs, P.O. Box 30552,
United Nations Avenue, Gigri, Nairobi, Kenya
http://www.unep.ch/

U.S. NATIONAL PARK SERVICE
1849 C Street NW, Washington, D.C. 20240
(202) 208-6843 http://www.nps.gov/

THE WILDERNESS SOCIETY
900 Seventh Street, NW,
Washington, D.C. 20006-2506
(202) 833-2300
http://www.wilderness.org/index.shtml

First edition for the United States, its territories and dependencies, Canada and the Philippine Republic, published 1999 by
Barron's Educational Series, Inc.
Original edition copyright © by 1999 Ticktock Publishing, Ltd.
U.S. edition copyright © 1999 by Barron's Educational Series, Inc.
All rights reserved. No part of this book may be reproduced in any form, by photostat, microfilm, xerography, or any other means, or incorporated
into any information retrieval system, electronic or mechanical, without the written permission of the copyright owner.
All inquires should be addressed to: Barron's Educational Series, Inc., 250 Wireless Boulevard, Hauppauge, New York 11788,
http://www.barronseduc.com
Library of Congress Catalog Card No. 98-74677
International Standard Book No. 0-7641-0640-6
Printed in Hong Kong
987654321

Picture Credits: t=top, b=bottom, c=center, l=left, r=right, OFC=outside front cover, OBC=outside back cover, IFC=inside front cover

Auscape; 8tl, 21c, 28bl. BBC Natural History Unit; 22cl. Bruce Colman Limited; 12bl, 20bl, 24tl. FLPA; 19bc, 29tl. NHPA; OFC (main pic)
15tl, 18b, 21br, 25tr, 24/25t, 26tl, 26bl. Oxford Scientific Films; IFC, 21 & OFC (inset), 2tc, 2b, 2/3c, 4tl, 4br, 4/5t, 4/5c, 5cr, 6tl, 8bc, 8bl, 8cl,
8/9c, 9b, 10tl, 10bl, 10/11bc, 11c, 13tl, 14l, 14/15c, 15b, 15c, 17tl, 17r, 18tl & OBC, 18/19t, 20/21b, 22bl, 22/23t, 22/23b & OBC, 23tr, 27cr,
31tr. Planet Earth; 5br, 6bl, 7br, 7tl, 9rc, 9tl, 10/11t & 32, 11br, 11tr, 12tl, 13b, 13tr, 14b, 14t, 16br, 16tl, 16tr, 17bl, 19cl, 19c, 19r, 20tl,
20/21t, 22tl, 24bl, 24/25r, 26/27c, 27br, 27tr, 28br, 30bl, 31c. SATC, Australian Tourist Commission; 28tl. Spectrum Colour Library; 28c,
30/31cb. Still Pictures; 3br, 29r, 30c, 30tl. Telegraph Colour Library; 7tr.

Every effort has been made to trace the copyright holders and we apologize in advance for any unintentional omissions.
We would be pleased to insert the appropriate acknowledgment in any subsequent edition of this publication.

BARRON'S